A Passion for Roses

J. C. SUARÈS

LAURA CERWINSKE

A WELCOME BOOK

ANDREWS AND McMEEL

KANSAS CITY

I saw a rosebud ope this morn: I'll swear
The blushing morning opened not more fair.

Abraham Cowley
THE SPRING

Into a little close of mine I went
>One morning when the sun with his fresh light
>was rising all refulgent and unshent.
Rose-trees are planted there in order bright.
>Whereto I turned charmed eyes, and long did stay,
>Taking my fill of that new-found delight.
Red and white roses bloomed upon the spray;
>One opened, leaf by leaf, to greet the morn,
Shyly, at first, then in sweet disarray;
>Another, yet a youngling, newly born,
>Scarce struggled from the bud, and there were some
>Whose petals closed them from the air forlorn;
Another fell, and showered the grass with bloom;
>Thus I behold the roses dawn and die,
>And one short hour their loveliness consume.

Lorenzo de' Medici

Keeping Roses Fresh

Before arranging the stems in a vase or bowl, immerse them in a container of room-temperature water and recut the ends at a 45-degree angle, one or two inches above the bottom. Cutting them under water prevents the formation of air bubbles, which can block the flow of nutrients up through the stem. The diagonal angle exposes the most stem to water and permits the flower to drink freely.

After cutting the stems, let the roses float in the water for at least half an hour. Then, after removing them, cut away any leaves or thorns that would be submerged in a vase or bowl. Their eventual decay would produce bacteria that can block the stem. Also, pare off any leaves above the surface, as these will draw off moisture before it can reach the blossoms.

Place the roses in a vase or bowl and add room-temperature water. Use hot water to force young buds open. Arrange the flowers, and place them out of direct sunlight.

The Biblical Rose

In one legend of Creation, a white rose and a lily flowered in Paradise. Adam asked Eve which of the two was the more beautiful. Eve sought the counsel of the Archangel Gabriel, who, it turned out, preferred the lily because the rose's thorns pricked him when he tried to pluck a bloom. Greatly offended, the rose left the garden at the same time Adam and Eve were driven out.

The Moral:
The fragrance of the rose should be reward enough.

Drying Roses

Materials

Fresh roses
String
Pipe cleaners
  (optional)
Wire coat hangers
  (optional)

Select a dark, dry place such as a closet or the attic. Take three or four stems and wind a pipe cleaner around them. The stems will shrink as they dry, so be certain to bind them tightly to prevent them from slipping out.

Tie one end of a piece of string to the twisted-together end of the pipe cleaner, and the other end to the horizontal bottom of a coat hanger.

One coat hanger will support four or five bunches of roses. Or, tie the bundle directly onto a roof beam or clothes rod. Either way, the roses should hang upside down.

You can also simply tie the stems with string, although pipe cleaners will enable you to remove one or two roses at a time and then rewind the others tightly until you're ready to display them.

14   *The Gallica, or French rose, is considered the oldest of the roses.*

She's the sweetest little rosebud that Texas ever knew,

Her eyes they shine like diamonds,

they sparkle like the dew.

You may talk about Clementine,

and sing of Rosalie,

But the Yellow Rose of Texas

the only girl for me.

Rose Curatives

Roman naturalist Pliny the Elder, author of *Historia Naturalis*, wrote in 77 A.D. that the rose could be used in the treatment of thirty-two health conditions, including infirmities of the stomach, sleeplessness, skin wounds, and inflammations of the eyes, ears, and mouth. The ancient Persians and Romans initiated the custom of dropping rose leaves into their wine to prevent or delay drunkenness. Much later, rose wine was prescribed in Elizabethan England to lift depression.

Medieval monks were so intent on perpetuating the use of roses that they cultivated gardens specifically for medicinal purposes. A staple of their apothecaries was dried *Rosa gallica* var. *officinalis*. In nineteenth-century Provins, France, the government warranted the use of rose salves in hospitals. Rose tea, brewed from rose petals and thyme, was used to soothe nerves, induce sleep, and cure colds. Petals of *Rosa damascena* were taken with honey to relieve coughing.

Candied rose petals—a healing delicacy—were treats that could cast away melancholy. A pomade made from rose petals and bear grease—a healing vanity—could be applied to the scalp to restore hair.

The rose hips of *Rosa canina* contain more vitamin C than any fruit. A rosehip syrup or capsule can be used as a nutritional supplement when citrus is unavailable.

> Go, lovely rose,
> Tell her that wastes her time and me
> That now she knows,
> When I resemble her to thee,
> How sweet and fair she seems to be.

Edmund Waller
Go, Lovely Rose

She drips herself with water and her shoulders
Glisten as silver, they crumple up
Like wet and falling roses, and I listen
For the sluicing of their rain disheveled petals.
In the window full of sunlight
Concentrates her golden shadow
Fold on fold, until it glows as
Mellow as the glory roses.

D.H. Lawrence
GLOIRE DE DIJON

24 *The middle name of Josephine, wife of Napoleon I, was Rose.*

The White Rose of the Orient

Once upon a time, a dispirited knight by the name of Sir Henry was returning to England after fighting in the Crusades. Stopping in Damascus to recover from his bloody adventures, he decided to visit the Gardens of Solomon. There the weary knight settled himself under a stand of cypress trees to watch the beautiful Saracen women pick the roses from which they would make precious oil. They carried huge baskets of red, pink, and white petals on their heads, never dropping any as they bent to their task.

✻ Among the rose pickers was a Persian slave girl named Sheramur, who sang a sweetly compelling song as she worked. Intoxicated as much by the melody as by her beauty, Henry beseeched her to sing for him alone. ✻ That evening, Sheramur came to Henry and sat at his feet, singing in an unbearably pure voice. Awed by the beauty of her mysterious words, Henry begged the girl to tell him the meaning of the song. "It is the legend of the birth of the red rose," she confided. "When the first white rose bloomed, the nightingale was seized with such love for the flower that he flung himself against it and was pierced with its thorns. As he lay dying upon its petals, his blood colored the white blossom a dark crimson, and so it has bloomed ever since." ✻ Entranced by Sheramur's delicate voice and alabaster skin, Sir Henry began to think of the girl herself as a white rose. He wondered whether the love-sacrifice of a bleeding heart would turn her into a crimson rose. But that night, having captured Sir Henry's love, Sheramur escaped into the dark and disappeared forever into the arms of her princely lover, leaving Sir Henry to die of a broken heart.

30 *In Christian iconography, a rose without thorns represents virtue.*

place shall be glad for them;
and blossom as the rose.

ISAIAH 35:1

A Recipe for Potpourri To Be Made in Early Summer

Initial Mixture:

3 pints rose petals (traditionally
  Rosa damascena, *Rosa gallica*,
  and Cabbage roses)
1 pint peony petals
1 pint clove carnation petals
1 pint sweet marjoram petals
  and leaves
$1/2$ pint lavender flowers
$1/2$ pint myrtle leaves
$1/2$ pint lemon verbena leaves
Rock salt

Additional Ingredients:

8 tablespoons brandy
2 tablespoons brown sugar
1 orange rind, powdered
1 lemon rind, powdered
8 dried bay leaves
$1/2$ oz. grated nutmeg
$1/2$ oz. powdered cloves
$1/2$ oz. orris
$1/2$ oz. allspice

Dry the flowers and leaves for two days. Then pour into a large pot and sprinkle with a handful of rock salt. Place a heavy plate on top to weigh the mixture down and encourage decomposition. Throughout the season, stir the mixture before adding additional layers. When the pot is nearly full, stir thoroughly and add another layer of salt. Replace the plate and let stand for two weeks until a "cake" forms. Crumble this and mix in additional spices. Replace the plate, cover, and let the potpourri mature. After six months, it will be ready to be poured into cache pots or decorative bowls. When its fragrance begins to wane, give it a stir, and add a few drops of rose oil.

There fell a silvery-silken veil of light,
With quietude, and sultriness, and slumber,
Upon the upturned faces of a thousand
Roses that grew in an enchanted garden,
Where no wind dared to stir, unless on tiptoe—
Fell on the upturn'd faces of these roses
That gave out, in return for the love-light,
Their odorous souls in an ecstatic death—
Fell on the upturn'd faces of these roses
That smiled and died in this parterre, enchanted
By thee, and by the poetry of thy presence.

Edgar Allan Poe
TO HELEN

Classification of Roses

There are three general classifications of roses: Old Garden Roses, Modern Roses, and Shrub Roses—a category created by the American Rose Society for a group of modern roses with large growth habits that do not fit into other classifications.

Old Garden Roses include the Alba, Bourbon, Centifolia, China, Damask, Eglanteria, Gallica, Hybrid Foetida, Hybrid Perpetual, Hybrid Spinosissima, Moss, Noisette, Portland, Species, and Tea Roses.

Modern Roses include the Hybrid Tea, Polyantha, Floribunda, Grandiflora, Miniature, Rambler, and Climber.

Shrub Roses include the Hybrid Moyesii, Hybrid Rugosa, Kordesi, Hybrid Musk, and a class simply known as Shrub.

Why is it no one ever sent me yet

One perfect limousine, do you suppose?

Ah no, it's always just my luck to get

One perfect rose.

Dorothy Parker
ONE PERFECT ROSE

Gather ye rosebuds while ye may,
Old Time is still a-flying;
And this same flower that smiles today,
Tomorrow will be dying.

Robert Herrick
TO THE VIRGINS, TO MAKE MUCH OF TIME

Arranging Roses

The presence of roses enhances the ephemeral beauty of a room, whether they are displayed as single buds in crystal vases, or as groups of full blooms massed in antique bowls. ✳ Many English decorators have long favored bouquets of full-blown roses, while designers of spare interiors often prefer minimal arrangements of a few long stems. Syrie Maugham, the English society hostess and decorator whose 1920s London drawing room was a sensation of modulated, creamy whites, removed the leaves from her white roses so only their alabaster petals remained. American decorators Mario Buatta and Sister Parrish, on the other hand, have reveled in vibrant bouquets of many colors. ✳ Regardless of whether an arrangement contains one or many shades, and whether its blooms are open or closed, the proportions of the vase or bowl should always be considered. Never dwarf the elegance of long-stemmed roses with a bulky vase, or diminish the beauty of an abundant bouquet by crowding the flowers into a diminutive bowl.

Rose Water

Since antiquity, when wealthy Romans customarily poured it into their fountains to perfume the air as a gesture of welcome, rose water has been used to titillate and soothe the senses. In addition to its olfactory benefits, rose water makes a superb tonic for refreshing the skin, especially if one has been out in the sun.

Enter, then, the Rose garden when the first sunshine sparkles in the dew,

and enjoy with thankful happiness one of the loveliest scenes of earth.

S. Reynolds Hole

WORLD FAMOUS ROSE GARDENS

THE BAGATELLE

in Paris, France, was originally part of an estate owned by Marie Antoinette and later by Napoleon I. It contains more than 10,000 rose bushes of more than 1,500 varieties.

MOTTISFONT ABBEY

in Hampshire, England, is a twelfth-century Augustinian Priory with old-fashioned roses growing inside its walled garden.

ROSETO DE ROMA

in Rome, Italy, is sited in a natural amphitheater and contains 4,000 bushes in groups of five against a backdrop of climbing roses.

WESTBROEKPARK

in The Hague, Netherlands, grows 20,000 plants, representing 350 varieties of roses planted in beds of different geometric configurations.

PARC DE LA GRANGE

in Geneva, Switzerland, is a three-tiered, octagonal rose garden with 12,000 plants of 200 varieties. The garden is illuminated at night, and often used as a stage for plays based on rose themes.

ROSALEDA DEL PARQUE DEL OESTE

in Madrid, Spain, offers one of the most impressive rose displays in a country with exceptional rose gardens in nearly every major city.

ZAKIR ROSE GARDEN in Chandigarh, India (known as the "City of Roses"), contains 60,000 plants. It has separate gardens for the celebration of rose festivals, the cultivation of roses with a high oil content or extreme scent, and laboratory experimentation, as well as 300 beds of exhibition variety roses, a garden for colored ramblers, and a moonlight garden with only pure white blooms.

VILLA REALE in Monza, Italy, is the headquarters of the Italian Rose Society. In its Rosarium grow 5,000 roses of 1,000 varieties.

SISSINGHURST CASTLE in Kent, England, has a garden designed with old and new roses by the famed Bloomsbury writer Vita Sackville-West.

BUTCHART GARDENS in Victoria, Canada, offers spectacular rose displays in a garden dug on the site of a former mine.

THE PEGGY ROCKEFELLER ROSE GARDEN in New York, New York, is designed in the English fashion with climbing roses on a central arbor and perimeter trellises. Beds of miniature roses, hybrid teas, and grandifloras are planted along the garden paths, and other varieties are also displayed.

Yet Ah, that Spring should vanish with the Rose!
That Youth's sweet-scented manuscript should close!

THE RUBÁIYÁT OF OMAR KHAYYÁM
As translated by Edward FitzGerald

And the rose like a nymph to the bath addressed,
Which unveiled the depth of her glowing breast,
Till, fold after fold, to the fainting air
The soul of her beauty and love lay bare....

> *Percy Bysshe Shelley*
> THE SENSITIVE PLANT

Roses at first were white,
Till they could not agree
Whether my Sappho's breast
Or they more white should be. . . .
But being vanquished quite,
A blush their cheeks bespread;
Since which, believe the rest,
The roses first came red.

Robert Herrick
HESPERIDES

Rose Oil

Two tons of rose petals are required to produce one kilogram of essential oil. The flower must be picked just as its petals are beginning to open fully. Rose oil is used in the "holy oil" with which British sovereigns are annointed at their coronation. For others who can afford the luxury of the costly essence, it provides an exceptional balm when poured into a cool bath.

O! how much more doth beauty beauteous seem
By that sweet ornament which truth doth give!
The rose looks fair, but fairer we it deem
For that sweet odor, which doth in it live.

William Shakespeare
SONNET 54

*The rose garden appeared
on tombs in Roman catacombs
as a symbol of paradise.*

Copyright © 1996 J.C. Suarès
Text © 1996 Laura Cerwinske
Managing editor: Jane R. Martin
Design assistance: Christy Trotter
All rights reserved. No part of this book may be used or reproduced in any manner whatsoever without written permission except in the case of reprints in the context of reviews.

For information write:
Andrews and McMeel
A Universal Press Syndicate Company
4900 Main Street
Kansas City, Missouri 64112

A Welcome Book
Welcome Enterprises, Inc.
575 Broadway
New York, NY 10012

Note: Every effort has been made to locate the copyright owners of the material used in the book. Please let us know if an error has been made, and we will make any necessary changes in subsequent printings.

Library of Congress Catalog Card Number: 95-80758
ISBN: 0-8362-1330-0

Printed in China by Toppan Printing Company
1 2 3 4 5 6 7 8 9 10

Illustration Credits. 32–33, 35, 36–37, 39: © Murray Alcosser. 4, 19, 42: Courtesy The Bettmann Archive. 27: © Lance Dane. 57: The Lover Crowned (detail), Jean-Honoré Fragonard, c.1771, © The Frick Collection, New York. 45: © Lizzie Himmel. 7, 13, 23, 31, 61: © Leslie Jean-Bart. 5, 11, 53, 63: © Mark Lyon. 64: © Kitigawa II/Superstock. 15: Courtesy The Kobal Collection. 43: Metro-Goldwyn-Mayer/Courtesy The Kobal Collection. 47: © David Phelps. 55: White Roses, Henri Fantin-Latour, 1875. Philadelphia Museum of Art: Bequest of Charlotte Dorrance Wright. Case cover, 20, 25, 28–29, 40: © Lanny Provo. 1: © Rivera Collection/Superstock. 8, 9: © Maria I. Robledo. 59: Josef Sudek/Courtesy Howard Greenberg Gallery, New York. 17: United Artists/Courtesy The Kobal Collection. 48–49: Warner Brothers/Courtesy The Kobal Collection. 2–3: © Elizabeth Watt.

Text Credits. 22: "Gloire de Dijon" from The Complete Poems of D.H. Lawrence, edited by V. de Sola Pinto and F.W. Robert. Copyright 1964, 1971 by Angelo Ravelgi and C.M. Weekly, Executors of the Estate of Freida Lawrence Roberts. Used by permission of Viking Penguin, a division of Penguin Books USA, Inc. 34: Potpourri recipe Copyright 1990 by Graham Rose and Peter King. 40: "One Perfect Rose" from The Portable Dorothy Parker. Copyright 1926, renewed 1954 by Dorothy Parker. All rights reserved. Reprint by permission of Viking Penguin, a division of Penguin Books USA, Inc.